T0021755

**HISTORY
FOR
PEACE
TRACTS**

How do we understand what was, grapple with
what is and prepare for what is likely to be,
as a nation, as a people, as a community,
as individuals?

This series is an attempt to address this question
by putting into print thoughts, ideas and
concerns of some of South Asia's most
seminal thinkers.

In memory of Kozo Yamamura (1934–2017)

Remaking the Citizen for New Times

History, Pedagogy and the Amar Chitra Katha

DEEPA SREENIVAS

LONDON NEW YORK CALCUTTA

The text in this volume is an updated edition of a
lecture delivered at the 2016 History for Peace
conference: The Idea of Nationalism.

Seagull Books, 2023

© Deepa Sreenivas, 2023

First published in volume form
by Seagull Books, 2023

ISBN 978 1 80309 287 4

British Library Cataloguing-in-Publication Data

A catalogue record for this book
is available from the British Library

Typeset by Seagull Books, Calcutta, India
Printed and bound by WordsWorth India,
New Delhi, India

CONTENTS

THE ARGUMENT

The Indian comic-book series Amar
Chitra Katha (ACK; Timeless picture
stories) was founded in 1967 with two
goals: to re-introduce Indian children to
the 'authentic' history of the nation and
to make this history relevant to the
project of shaping the future citizen. This
was a monumental task, but its
remarkable success points to the
intersections or close imbrications of the
present and our re-imaginations of the
past, especially in the domain of the
popular. In this essay, I argue that the

value system the ACK so painstakingly crafted continues to animate the present even when the series is nowhere near as popular as it used to be in print form and has an entirely different life in digital spaces.

THE FOUNDING MYTH

While watching a quiz on Doordarshan, Anant Pai realized to his despair that the young participants from prestigious colleges and universities, while well informed about figures from Greek mythology, failed to answer simple questions on Indian mythology and history. This realization, pointing to the alienation of the youth from 'Indian' culture, led Pai to resign from a secure job as a journalist at the *Times of India* and launch a series of comic books titled Amar Chitra Katha in 1967, an initiative that took on the task of re-narrating myths, historical events, classics, legends and folk tales from India to its children. In a market inundated by American comics, this venture had a precarious future. Pai faced considerable setbacks in the initial days, with sales dipping and bookstores refusing to stock titles that were not associated with established comic brands. Schools would not buy these books for their libraries because comics were bracketed as frivolous reading material that would corrupt children's minds (and grammar). There are accounts of Pai struggling to sell his books during the early days, even personally peddling ACK titles at petrol-pump kiosks.

But the struggle would soon pay off, and the series would go on to make publishing history in India. Attractively produced, colourfully illustrated and reasonably priced, Amar Chitra Katha issues would soon become part and parcel of middle-class urban homes, valued as the kind of reading material essential for the proper upbringing of the child. Parents would take care to have the issues carefully bound, so that they could serve as an encyclopaedia of Indian history and mythology for the children, but also for older members of the family.

However, a closer look at the circumstances surrounding the birth of the ACK unravel connections that go beyond the passion and drive of a single individual, situating it instead in a complex web of cultural and political shifts in the late 60s and early 70s. The ACK came into existence at a historical conjuncture of the Nehruvian state's increasingly visible contradictions and inequalities. As historians and political commentators have widely discussed, the exuberance and hope that marked the Nehruvian era soon grew into a sense of discontent among various sections of people. The promise of social and economic justice remained unmet, and the bureaucratized, top-down mechanism of planning and development failed to take into account the immediate, local contexts of people's lives. By the late 60s, economic growth slowed down and prices soared. Widespread disillusionment with the state and its policies and lingering feudal structures of oppression led to an explosion of protests, including militant struggles, by socially and economically marginalized groups—women, workers, peasants and tribal groups.[1]

Alongside radical uprisings against dominant groups, a distinct set of challenges surfaced from the right, blaming the twin ideologies closely associated with the Nehruvian state, secularism and socialism, for the moral collapse of the nation and calling for a spiritual revolution in their place.[2] Closely aligned with the position of the right was an emergent domestic bourgeoisie that was already forging crucial partnerships with foreign capital by the mid-70s. Oriented towards the ethic of competitive individualism, this middle class held the welfarist policies of the state responsible for the economic stagnation and devaluation of merit. It demanded a masculinization of the self in place of 'special rights' guaranteed by the Constitution to historically marginalized groups. The ACK inserts itself into this discourse of the right by fashioning a nationalist, brahminized yet modern masculinity as the model for emulation by middle-class children.

Promising to counter the influence of the West on the youth, it seeks to revive the 'authentic' traditions of India through a re-telling of history and mythology, colourfully illustrated in a chitra-katha (picture story) format. The ACK can today claim to have moulded the ideas

concerning nation and the citizen of
children growing up in the 70s and 80s,
and shaped their 'aspirational'
articulations of merit, hard work and
self-respect.[3]

CULTURAL NEGOTIATIONS

For dominant groups to maintain their
moral and political leadership, Antonio
Gramsci argued, they must re-articulate
their goals and politics by connecting with
the beliefs, aspirations, fears and emotions
of the rest of society. In this process, they
may have to give up some of their
interests, while still holding on to their
'core' norms. The dominant class, then,
should not be seen as uniformly repressive
or wholly coercive. A great deal of work
and negotiation goes into maintaining its
dominance, or, as Gramsci terms it,
hegemony.[4]

A hegemonic 'text', such as the Amar Chitra Katha, addresses these cultural concessions and contradictions in society; it may even be critical of certain dominant practices, but it simultaneously firms up an 'essence' of the nation/community that is unchangeable, often by tracing an unbroken link between the present and a singular, glorious past. This process is never complete—there are always opposing pressures and alternative articulations in civil society that must be countered or re-aligned with safer, more acceptable formulations (or discourses) such that its disruptive potential is contained. For a cultural text to be powerful, it must continuously respond to and re-articulate contemporary concerns and discontents.

Through their promise to make history 'fun' and their efforts to consciously distance themselves from the dates-and-facts approach of the school history textbook, the ACK re-authenticated certain dominant cultural norms and reclaimed a universal status for them during a critical phase of the nation. Furthermore, the ACK trained generations of upper-caste middle-class children to internalize and embody the ideals of perseverance, excellence and merit. More than half a century after the series was established, these norms continue to form a critical foundation of the hegemony of the upper-caste middle-class in India.

I recall starting my engagement with the ACK with a rather straightforward intent: to look at it as an innovation in the field of children's writing that borrows from the Western comic format to retell stories from the Indian past. But that objective did not quite work out, for reasons to be discussed.

MERIT UNDER THREAT

The 1990s were marked by intense debates around the idea of merit and its presumed neutrality. In August 1990, when the then prime minister V. P. Singh announced his decision to implement the recommendations of the Mandal Commission Report (1980)—to institute reservations for the Other Backward Classes in government services and public-sector jobs, in addition to the already-existing reservations for Scheduled Castes and Tribes—there were country-wide agitations by upper-caste groups that frequently turned violent. Students from upper-caste middle-class sections voiced their protest in the language of meritocracy. They were convinced that caste-based reservations would impede the progress of the nation, breeding inefficiency in the public sector.

The language of meritocracy, then and now, acquires legitimacy in two ways: one, by not wading into the historical marginalization of certain groups that underlies the logic of affirmative action; and two, by co-opting and re-envisaging equality as a condition which is genuinely achieved only when caste, class and gender identity are transcended. Yet, during the anti-Mandal agitations, when pro-merit agitators adopted street-sweeping or shoe-shining as modes of protest, they inadvertently revealed the hidden class/caste affiliations of the avowedly secular, middle-class meritocratic self. At that historical moment, especially within university spaces, one was pushed to engage with the overt and covert presence of caste in institutions and disciplines, in textbooks and in classrooms.

During the events of the 90s, it became clear that political theory and other humanist discourse has often described and based itself on a notion of a human essence that is ahistorical and unchanging. Gender, class and caste are merely incidental and part of the contingencies of the social realm: there is a human core beneath all the layers of identity. But this perspective conceals the historical and cultural construction of our politics itself.[5]

In this regard, I will interpret the Amar Chitra Katha as a cultural project that imbued middle-class India with the authority of caste, while simultaneously rendering it casteless.

THE PAST IN THE PRESENT

Tejaswini Niranjana has pointed out how the earlier colonialist as well as nationalist descriptions of society were premised on a separation between culture and modernity 'so that culture lay in the past and modernity was simply the time-space within which the leaving behind of culture was manifested.'[6] This distinction drew from the orientalist ideologies that described 'Indian culture' as antiquated and unchanging, resistant to modernity due to religious beliefs and superstitions. The nationalists would counter this perception through a rearticulation, highlighting the glorious spiritual and artistic traditions of India's ancient culture—distinct from its sluggish, superstition-ridden present on the one hand, and the depraved, materialistic modernity of the colonizer on the other. However, cultural studies in India takes shape through a critique of such descriptions, both orientalist and nationalist, by 'challenging the separation between culture and modernity.'[7] In this framework, culture is seen as implicated in our contemporary contexts and politics, shaping as well as shaped by everyday experiences, practices and institutions.

I make two claims premised on such a reconceptualization of culture: (a) the Amar Chitra Katha's history and mythology have a contemporary frame of reference, and (b) in order to make this past effective in the present, it radically breaks from the fact-based textbook notion of history. Its pedagogic and citizen-making endeavour remains closely engaged with cultural politics.

The ACK is strategically situated in a domain considered to be apolitical—children's literature—and thus, beyond the concerns of politics and adults. I have discussed elsewhere how childhood has been hegemonically constructed in children's narratives, textbooks, consumer culture and popular media as a period of innocence, play, spontaneity and vulnerability—clearly marked off from the adult world of responsibility and work.[8] However, a probing of the dominant ideal of childhood uncovers its middle-class and upper-caste affiliations, unsettling its claim to universality. Perry Nodelman has shown how writers and publishers of children's literature make judgements about what to produce based not on what they believe will appeal to children but, rather, on what adult consumers (parents, teachers, guardians, librarians) *believe* will appeal to them.[9]

In 2016, I presented a version of this essay at the History for Peace conference. It was more than 25 years since the tumultuous 90s that turned upside down an innocuous children's comic series for me. However, a more immediate event led me to reconnect with this research. On 17 January 2016, just a few months before the seminar, Rohith Vemula, a Dalit scholar pursuing research in one of the premiere public universities of the country, committed suicide. The tragic death of this young man, articulate, well read, aspiring to be a writer on science like Carl Sagan, yet reaching the decision that death alone would allow him to travel from 'shadows to the stars',[10] led many within the academia to confront the idea of merit and the many contradictions and privileges underpinning it. Once again, we struggled with the questions: Who can claim merit? Who is the ideal citizen? Who has the cultural confidence to belong and what is this confidence made of? Who falls by the wayside?

This was therefore an appropriate time to revisit the brief history of 'merit' that I had traced through my engagement with the ACK and the cultural labour that constructs merit, dissociated from caste, gender or community.

Since the fateful tragedy of Rohith's death, we have witnessed many more suicides by students from marginalized communities in prestigious institutions of higher education in India. As Ajantha Subramanian notes, the formal and legal equality of individuals in liberal democratic societies works as a smokescreen to erase collective histories of privilege and exclusion.[11] Further, such a perspective presents the individual as the bearer of innate capacities; it individualizes and naturalizes merit, delinking it from systemic advantages.

REGRESSIVE MODERNIZATION

The Amar Chitra Katha assumes the task of constructing the culturally rooted, modern Indian citizen. Its creator Anant Pai's attempt to refashion history—which he presents as a series of vignettes of the heroism and charisma of great men and (a few) women—into an effective pedagogic tool stands in distinct contrast to other contemporary but radical historiographical initiatives, such as subaltern studies that emerged in the early 80s and critiqued the elitist basis of both colonial and nationalist historiography. One may well characterize the ACK, with its accent on the moral rejuvenation of the youth by reconnecting them with their traditions, as a powerful initiative of 'regressive modernization', borrowing from Stuart Hall's incisive analysis of conservative discourse during the Thatcher era.[12] This discourse, better known as Thatcherism, repeatedly invoked the lost glories of the British Empire and the loss of its colonies to legitimize its aspiration for a white, masculinized middle-class identity.

Cultural theorists have drawn attention to the subjectivities of extraordinary, resilient and agentive protagonists that emerged in the literature and cinema of the 70s. Susie Tharu and K. Lalita unpack the reappearance of the Hindu widow in the fiction of the post-

Independence era. In M. K. Indira's award-winning novel *Phaniyamma* (1976), the protagonist is an upper-caste widow who observes traditional rituals in their strictest austerity and yet demonstrates the humane face of tradition when she breaks caste taboo by assisting a lower-caste woman in childbirth. A critique of Nehruvian secularism underwrites such representations, throwing into sharp relief the latter's disconnect from 'Indian values'. Tharu and Lalita note: 'The narrative carefully sifts out the "good, mature" rewriting of tradition in the larger interests of society and of the nation, from the selfish or self-centred "immature" rebellions, just as it distinguishes between the harsh and superstitious practice of ritual and a deep, rational adherence to tradition.'[13] Significantly, Pai imagines the ACK as a substitute for the grandmother who through her storytelling kept the children connected to their 'roots', but was fast disappearing with the disintegration of joint families in urban settings.

The right's ideological labour in the 70s was directed at a 'moral regeneration of the society', shifting the focus from struggles waged from the margins. The ACK's insistence on a valorized, authentic Indian past must be seen within this context. However, it would be reductive to completely bracket the ACK within the ideology of Hindu nationalism or right-wing politics: its ingenuity lies in pulling together the idea of the Hindu nation and secularism into a seamless articulation. Within its worldview, everyone who shares the 'core' values of the nation qualifies for its membership, irrespective of caste or community. When the Muslim is excluded from the idea of the nation, it is because he deviates from 'our' norms and values. The epitome of the recalcitrant, aberrant Muslim in the ACK, as in many Hindu majoritarian discourses, is Alauddin Khilji, a threat to the chastity of the Rajput queen Padmini and, by extension, the purity of the nation and its women.

THE RIGHT ROUTE
TO OUR 'ROOTS'[14]

The Amar Chitra Katha draws on many
foundational premises of Hindutva: the
Rashtriya Swayamsevak Sangh's
organicist model in which the individual
is conceived as a cell of a larger social
body, with all traces of free will repressed
through rigid discipline; or the Jana
Sangh's re-imagining of Hinduization as
Indianization, standing for the cultural
oneness of India. Balraj Madhok, an
ideologue of the Jana Sangh, in his
widely circulated *Indianisation* (1970),

emphasized the cultural singularity of India which for him was synonymous with Hindu culture, founded on a Vedic philosophy. Madhok also appealed for changes to school textbooks which, he felt, distorted facts by erasing references to India's traditional (and Hindu) heroes and heroines in the name of secularism.

The ACK was launched a few years following the founding of the Vishva Hindu Parishad (VHP) in 1964. Its narratives clearly address the cultural anxieties experienced in the rank and file of the VHP, specifically the need for the 'modern guru' who can bring back the Westernized middle class to the folds of Hinduism. In the words of its ideologue, Swami Chinmayananda (a self-stylized 'modern guru'):

> A new type of swami is emerging
> in this country who will serve as
> missionatries [*sic*] to their own
> people. At this crucial time of our
> history, we do not need those who
> live in a cave and meditate.[15]

The historical and mythological protagonists of the ACK are shaped as teachers/leaders for the present, demonstrating a contiguity and harmony with the vision of the VHP.[16]

The figure of an ordinary child with extraordinary potential has been a motif in the ACK since the publication of its first issue *Krishna* in 1969. While the child Krishna displays divine powers, he also remains an ordinary boy, with the illustrations shoring up such a double effect. As Krishna is shown dancing on the hood of the deadly snake Kaliya, a crowd of onlookers from the village gather to watch him in wonder, their backs turned to the reader/viewer. But two of them turn to face the rest (and the reader). 'What a boy!' says one of them, with an expression of indulgent bemusement, his tone 'personalized'.

As Anuradha Kapur has observed: 'What happens when the story is about gods and heroes from epics? The personalized tone of voice and causality of the narrative "secularizes" the event and makes the action plausible in human terms. Thus, gods and heroes appear understandable to us, close to us, like us.'[17]

Krishna is represented, on the one hand, as an ideal, and on the other, he invites identification and emulation from the child reader/viewer by producing a sense of familiarity.

In the process of reconstructing the past, the ACK blurs the boundary between history and popular culture. Shrewdly assessing the popularity of Superman and Phantom comics in the India in the 60s and 70s, Pai understood that he needed to pitch his content in that very domain if it were to find a toehold in the thriving market. We know that the comic, since its inception, especially since the 50s, has been viewed with suspicion by parents and educators the world over. Which leads us to the question: How did Pai adapt this medium as a vehicle for fulfilling the lofty aim of teaching 'Indian themes and values' to children? His own response is illuminating:

In all fairness, it must be admitted that some comics could do damage to the impressionable minds of children. If there are bad comics, let us oppose them, as we oppose bad books or bad movies, but let us not frown on comics as a medium of education. Should we stop using a tool as useful as a comic, just because it can cause harm? A matchbox is useful—a must for every house. Do we stop using it because it can cause a fire?[18]

The Amar Chitra Katha adapts many formalistic features from the comic but carves its own distinct form also. It combines the comic format with the lavish visual traditions of the katha, chitra katha and scrolls, traditional narrative modes from various regions of India that speak of the grand conquests and adventures of kings and princes.[19] One may well ask: How can something so extravagant pass for history? I have argued elsewhere that despite its grandeur and mythologized history, the ACK remains rooted in contemporary frames of reference. The hero might be Krishna or Shivaji or Jayaprakash Narayan, but he is emblematic of what an individual *can* become if he strives to realize his fullest potential.

Each comic, while about the past, also serves as an allegory for the imagined community of the nation. In *Padmini* (1973), Ratnasen is represented as the good-hearted yet gullible king who, in a fatal error of judgement, trusts Alauddin Khilji when he expresses brotherly sentiments towards his queen Padmini, thus paving the way for the cunning Sultan to usurp his palace and the kingdom of Chittor. Padmini commits jauhar (ritual self-immolation) to save her 'honour'.[20] A careful reading of this re-presentation of the Padmini myth uncovers the underlying subtext of Partition, forever projected as an act of betrayal by Muslims in the hegemonic nationalist imagination.[21] Ratnasen is good but weak-hearted, an appeaser for a leader. The narrative/visual strategies barely present him as significant enough to be a model for emulation like many other Rajput heroes in the ACK. If we read this in the larger context of right-wing ideology that consistently accuses Nehruvian secularism of minority appeasement, the king Ratnasen mirrors the premier Nehru.

IMBRICATIONS

Pai emphasizes the instructive rather than informative potential of history—a strategy similar to that of the nineteenth-century Bengali man of letters, Bankim Chandra Chatterjee. In his historical fiction, Chatterjee sets up the magic, colour and inventiveness of history-as-story against the 'meaningless jumble of dates and names of persons and places'.[22]

As Sudipta Kaviraj points out, the writing of nationalist history followed two different trajectories: the real and the imaginary. The former was marked by factual research; the latter by a fictive imagination turning to historical subjects.[23] Significantly, at a point when James Mill disqualified 'oriental fables' from the domain of rational history, many proponents of rationalism such as Bankim Chandra and Romesh Chunder Dutt combined 'real' and 'imaginary' histories. The indigenous historian inserted Puranic myths, legends and romances into the historical discourse.

Mimicking the example of Bankim Chandra (and the prominent trend of nationalist history in the nineteenth century), the boundaries of community within the 'fictional' history of the Amar Chitra Katha remained fluid and allowed anybody—avowedly irrespective of caste or community—to become a part of the imagined community of the nation. Within this frame, an allegiance to the memory of Padmini's 'sacrifice' or Shivaji's 'vanquishment of Muslim invaders' or the valour of Rana Pratap becomes the touchstone for the patriotism of every Indian, whatever region, caste or community s/he may belong to. A Rajput identity is conflated with 'Indian' identity, the history of Rajasthan represents the glorious past of India. To cite from the introduction to *Rana Pratap* (1977): 'In essence Rana Pratap's name is synonymous to the highest order of the revolutionary patriotic spirit of India.'[24]

Exemplifying the triumph of the individual in the most trying circumstances, the ACK's narratives serve as an elaborate practical guide for modern middle-class children in a competitive, globalizing world. It is difficult to miss the crucial link between the ACK and Pai's prescriptions for the development of 'personality'—a term resonant with the modern connotations of leadership and communication skills. This leads me to the Partha Institute of Personality Development, founded by Pai in the 80s. This initiative is far from being as well-known as the ACK, but it is important to trace the contiguities between both projects.

PARTHA AND PERSONALITY

'Personality', in an entrepreneurial, corporate context, connotes attributes such as appearance, enterprise, confidence, ambition and the drive to deal with challenges and succeed. Pai sets up an interesting traffic between history and the discourse of personality development, with history envisioned as a pedagogic tool to teach children how not to fail, and how to be confident citizens in a competitive, individualist world. Emerging on the eve of the 70s, the Amar Chitra Katha had its finger on the pulse of the palpable discontent brewing among the younger generation, faced with the increasing pressures of education and the prospect of unemployment. In addition, there was a rising disillusionment with the iconic figures of nationalist discourse.[25] Pai speaks of the time when he witnessed 'educated youngsters of Bombay resorting to violence'. He writes, 'I then met and talked to many youngsters and realized that though today's education imparts a lot of information to young minds, it does not prepare them to face life.'[26] Advertisements for enrolment into the Partha Institute of Personality Development appeared in various issues of the ACK, addressing parents in the following manner: 'The world is becoming increasingly competitive [. . .] Is your child prepared for the grim battle of survival and success? Just imparting him the three Rs (Reading, Writing, Arithmetic) is not enough. It is vital that he possesses the three Cs (character, confidence, courage) also.' A bridge is thus set up between the past and the present, between heroes of the ACK tales and the (globally) successful capitalist entrepreneurs.[27]

> History tells us of many great men who had very humble beginnings. Chandragupta Maurya, who founded the Mauryan Empire was a person of humble origin. Shalivahana, who established a mighty kingdom, was a potter's son! Kalidasa was

a shepherd boy. Sher Shah Suri, who defeated Humayun and became the Sultan of Delhi, was the son of a horse breeder of Sasaram. Hasan, who later became a popular ruler and was known as Bahman Shah, worked on the farm of a Brahmin called Gangu. Shivaji was the son of a petty chieftain.[28]

In the 80s and 90s, the ACK's practical middle-class ethic became increasingly geared towards fashioning a global Hindu identity. Pai draws from a range of sources to make this ethic viable and teachable to young people. An ethic resonant with Bankim Chandra's formulation of 'anushilan'—seeking the cultivation of innate human faculties, physical and intellectual—animates the ACK's imagination of an India where the culturally empowered Hindu with a global vision replaces the subject of the welfare state. Pai's stated claim that education should inculcate courage, patience, perseverance and a sense of fellowship in an individual,[29] skilfully re-notates the four virtues advocated by Bankim as essential for the Hindu male: enterprise, solidarity, courage and perseverance.[30] The ACK narratives also draw on Vivekananda's reframing of brahminism as a norm of excellence rather than as a status related to the 'accidents' of birth or caste. In *Adi Shankara* (1974), an 'outcaste' questions Shankara, refusing to move out of his path as customary: 'What shall I move?

My body of common clay or my soul of all-pervading consciousness?' Shankara then acknowledges his superiority: 'He has seen the one reality in all. He is indeed my guru, regardless of his low birth.'[31]

The pedagogic ingenuity of the ACK lies in seamlessly suturing the discourses of Bankim Chandra, Vivekananda or the Gita to that of the popular propagators of capitalist and corporate success in the West—Dale Carnegie and Ayn Rand. It imbues the capitalist worldview with moral authority, teaching modes of cultural leadership to middle-class children that fit in with a corporatized, globalized world and yet remain organically connected with 'tradition'.

In the Amar Chitra Katha, the implicit critique of welfarism and a plea for individualism is displaced onto a moral plane through the presentation of an ideal evolved self who has a responsibility to society. Drawing on figures such as Vivekananda, ACK ensures that the figure of the 'economic man' is not central to its discourse, and it is the duty of the educated upper-caste individual to educate the lower castes. In this manner, the individualist self, imbued with moral authority, replaces the interventionist state.

Chanakya (1971) demonstrates how a ruler must be carefully chosen and trained if he were to lead the nation with requisite power and authority. Chanakya, a celibate sage, trains Chandragupta

Maurya to become a mighty ruler. Visually represented as sinewy, muscular and powerful, Chanakya is not a reclusive hermit who meditates in caves, withdrawn from the world. Slighted by Nanda and faced with the invasion of Magadha by Alexander, he chooses Chandragupta—to overthrow the ruler. Chandragupta is anointed to be the new king as he is 'very brave, very intelligent and very powerful', with the right amount of respect for brahminical authority and order. Read against the backdrop of the 70s, *Chanakya* conveys that the ideal ruler must ally himself with the brahminical-patriarchal order.[32]

Notably, Babasaheb Ambedkar, the rallying point for Dalit politics, is also represented in an individualist and Hindu patriarchal mode in an eponymous issue devoted to him (1979).[33] The heroes of the ACK are routinely born at an auspicious hour in the Hindu calendar, signalling their extraordinary destiny. Hindu religious symbols fill the large opening panel of *Babasaheb Ambedkar*, as an ascetic prophecies Ambedkar's birth to his father: 'I bless you. You shall have a son, who will achieve worldwide fame.'

In the course of the narrative, we tour the gamut of Babasaheb's experiences—the struggle of his family to educate him, his solitary studies at two in the night in the crowded one-room tenement in Bombay, his endless hours of toil at the British Museum library in London. Each event is pressed into re-affirming the power of the individual, never allowing caste to emerge as a social and political question. In the manner of all ACK heroes, Ambedkar is a model of excellence. Most importantly, he emerges as an icon of merit. If we read this in the larger context of the ACK's valorization of the individual, the story hegemonically recasts the historical marginalization of the lower castes as a condition requiring 'meritorization' and self-elevation for emancipation. While Ambedkar's life and writings are foundational to Dalit politics and movements for reclaiming rights, in the ACK, this figure is deftly displaced on to a discourse that is fundamentally opposed to the special rights that the state is constitutionally obligated to provide to historically disadvantaged sections.

Babasaheb Ambedkar can be situated at the cusp of the cultural politics signalling the transition into the 80s. Significantly, it was republished in 1996 after the violent anti-Mandal agitations of the early 90s and the subsequent resurgence of Ambedkarite politics.

THE CURRENT MOMENT

As I return to my analysis of the Amar
Chitra Katha, three decades since I
engaged with it first, I wonder if its
worldview still has relevance? In the
early 90s, the popularity of the series
began waning. Pai had blamed the spread
of television for the dipping sales.
Nandini Chandra points to the ACK's
foray into the diaspora market with its
decline in the domestic market:

> The mid-1980s' marketing
> strategy of ACK was dominated
> by the single special issues in

threes and tens, like the *Dashavatara*, deluxe-bound versions of 10 titles, and mini-series based on the *Ramayana* and *Mahabharata*. All these special issues were in effect a repackaging of old issues for a more affluent market, but also designed with a strict Hindu accent.[34]

India Book House (IBH), the original publishers of ACK, clearly found themselves out of their depth competing with the global animation industry and online content. In 2007, this brand of classic comics changed hands from IBH to ACK Media, with the latter focused on making them available in multiple formats including print, DVD, digital content, games, podcasts and film, with a firm eye on the diaspora market. Clearly, ACK does not have a central hold on the urban, middle-class imagination any more and has to compete with a plethora of content. However, I would argue that its carefully constructed ethical norms continue to animate our present and remain foundational to the common sense of the globalized middle class.

CANONIZING SUCCESS

The normative moral order constructed
by Amar Chitra Katha—delinking the
ideas of merit and success from caste and
privilege—continues to be foundational,
underlying the symbols and practices that
establish Indian/Hindu identity. As Suhas
Palshikar notes, in the current political
context, the discourses of Hindutva and
development are woven together with
nationalism. 'The imagination of "new
India" is being developed in which the
emphasis is on opportunity and
achievement, thus replacing key reference

points such as welfare and redistribution.'[35] The slogans and ideas associated with popular campaigns such as the Swachh Bharat (Clean India), Make in India and Skill India centre a citizenly self that is responsible, nationalist and proud. The Swachh Bharat Mission, for instance, invokes the spirit of volunteerism and civic duty towards public hygiene among citizens. Aman Luthra points out how these campaigns reproduce colonial and postcolonial narratives of hygiene as a 'cultural problem', founded on the premise of a pre-modern Indian who needs to schooled in the practices of cleanliness: 'By focusing only on behaviour change (e.g. anti-littering), these campaigns privilege an understanding of waste as an aesthetic problem rather than a much more complicated infrastructural one.'[36] I believe that these narratives invoke the reformist citizen self that cultural initiatives like the ACK instituted—one who could intervene in 'social problems' (hunger, poverty, untouchability) without addressing fundamental social hierarchies.[37] Significantly, the ACK in recent years has associated itself with issues of ecology, climate change and recyclism. Its website greets us on World Environment Day and Nature Conservation Day with infographics alerting us to the significance of these events. On 15 March 2021, it introduced us to five women environmentalists from different regions—Tulsi Gowda, Almitra

Patel, Rahibai Popere, Saalumarada Thimmakka and Licypriya Kangujam.[38] On 15 December 2020, its website listed five books (with brief summaries) that are must reads for 'eco-warriors'—which included Amitav Ghosh's *The Hungry Tide* and Ruskin Bond's 'No Room for a Leopard'.[39] In 2017, a special edition titled *Swachh Bharat: The Clean Revolution*, with messages on sanitation and cleanliness aimed at school children and youth, was released following a memorandum between ACK Media and the Ministry of Urban Development.[40] The ACK, in its new avatar, straddles a range of discourses (internationally recognized authors, governmental campaigns) to address the 'new' citizen.

Contemporary critical discussions have unpacked how caste is presented as the antithesis of merit. I recall how ACK's collaboration with the Partha Institute of Personality Development worked to consolidate such an understanding. Subramanian notes, 'At the first glance, the two terms appear antithetical. Caste is a social institution most emblematic of ascriptive hierarchy, while meritocracy is typically understood as a democratizing force that levels inherited privileges and disadvantages.'[41] However, as Subramanian goes on to show, seven decades after Independence, caste and merit continue to share an intimate relationship in institutional spaces. For instance, the Indian Institutes of Technology (IITs), regarded as the bastions of merit, remain overwhelmingly upper caste in composition. Further, policies of affirmative action, which offer a limited amount of scope to those from socially marginalized backgrounds to access these spaces, are met with fervent resistance by the dominant castes in the name of protecting 'merit'.

What renders the meritocratic, successful 'new' middle class casteless, and thus, imbued with authority and legitimacy? Much more affluent, consumerist and transnational than the older middle class that Pai addressed in the 70s and 80s, this class has developed modes of self-fashioning that straddle the rhetoric of globalization and certain older middle-class values simultaneously. Through a study of a highly visible section of the Indian middle class, the employees of the information technology industry

(IT), Carol Upadhya provides us with interesting insights. Many of the software professionals she interviewed expressed a sense of national pride in how their role in the IT industry has facilitated India's prominent position in the global economy: 'The passion for entrepreneurship has been stimulated by the success stories of companies such as Infosys as well as NRI tech entrepreneurs such as Vinod Khosla and Kanwal Rekhi, who are role models for aspiring software engineers, symbolizing what Indians can achieve as entrepreneurs if the economy is freed by liberalization.'[42] In many of these stories, entrepreneurial achievements are firmly linked not to inherited wealth (as with an earlier business class) but with talent, hard work and professional excellence. The media hype around the co-founder of the

IT giant Infosys, Narayana Murthy, constantly highlights his simplicity and down-to-earth style, dedication and nationalist spirit alongside the global success of his entrepreneurial venture. Anas Rahman Junaid, the founder and managing director of the wealth-research agency Hurun India, feels that school syllabi must include a subject on entrepreneurship. Reminding us of how Pai bridged the gap between history and fun, Junaid feels that such learning should not merely be an academic exercise: 'It'll be interesting if someone can put together comic books around entrepreneurship and business to create interest among children at an early age—something like an Amar Chitra Katha. That should do wonders.'[43]

Significantly enough, in recent years, ACK Media has been commissioned by top business houses of India to write about their journeys in special edition issues. In 2019, *The Tata Story* was published by ACK Media, tracing the rise of the Tatas. As the *Hindu BusinessLine* notes, this is the first time that the media house has published an illustrated book on corporates in its history spanning fifty years.[44] In 2022, ACK Media partnered with Godrej & Boyce to publish a book about industrialist Naval Godrej: *Naval Godrej: Pioneer of Progress*. The words of Preeti Vyas, the current president and CEO of ACK Media, combine the trademark the ACK register of nation building and individual grit with a more contemporary register (for instance, 'atmanirbharta'):[45]

> The Naval Godrej story is one of determination, innovation and above all deep love for India. This

story is indeed one of nation-building, and is so apt in today's context, where India strives towards self-reliance and atmanirbharta in all fields. Growing up in a globalised world, Indian children today need inspirational stories of Indian innovators and entrepreneurs who worked hard to make India self-reliant and put us on the global map with their determination and innovation.[46]

I had earlier discussed how Pai had re-notated Bankim Chandra's idea of anushilan to imbue entrepreneurship with spiritual authority. In the current entrepreneurial/IT context, certain foundational brahminical norms are re-articulated with immense purchase in a global corporate world that values efficiency, integrity and transparency as professional ethics.[47] Upadhya notes how a senior IT professional who she interviewed felt 'purity of behaviour' was a truly Indian value and cited Rama's actions in the Ramayana as illustrative of this purity: 'The conflation of corporate ethics, middle-class identity and Indian religiosity in the self-representation of these companies indicates how closely these diverse discourses are imbricated in one another, as also the Brahminical orientation of the industry.'[48]

CONCLUDING THOUGHTS

This essay has looked at how the Amar Chitra Katha was central to the self-fashioning of an urban, globalizing middle class from the 70s to the present day. Its historiography remained closely engaged with culture—drawing both its form and content from the mythologies, legends and visuality embedded in our everyday worlds. It linked ideas such as success, achievement and wealth creation to the innate moral superiority of an individual and thus effectively displaced an earlier welfarist ethic. As several scholars have pointed out, a range of cultural initiatives have worked to consolidate a masculine, individualist persona in the 80s and 90s. Kajri Jain and Anuradha Kapur have traced the emergence of a muscular Ram during the Ram Janmabhoomi movement, always alone, unaccompanied by Sita or Lakshman, unlike in traditional iconography such as the bazaar prints or calendars.[49] According to Jain, these masculine images reclaimed the space generated by Amitabh Bachchan's angry-young-man persona—an embodiment of the class and caste disillusionment with the state in 70s and 80s—and worked this image on to a safer, more conservative terrain. Television series such as *Mahabharata* and *Ramayana*, telecasted by Doordarshan during the late 80s and early 90s, significantly shored up the upper-caste Hindu identity, centring a brahminical world order. Purnima Mankekar observes how this period has been a critical point in postcolonial Indian history, 'when constructions of nation were rearticulated and religious identities renegotiated.'[50] Uma Chakravarti discusses how the masculine self was re-imagined in the televised serial *Chanakya* by representing its eponymous protagonist as the archetype of masculine authority: 'In the far-reaching reinterpretation of *Dharma* (duty), the patriotic worshipper of nation could lie, cheat, bribe, and incite the cause of Dharma where Dharma now stood for securing the integrity, unity, and Brahminic values of the nation.'[51]

In many ways, the ACK anticipates and in fact prepares an environment for the cultural projects cited above. But there is something distinct about the ACK; emerging on the cusp between the Nehruvian era and a more market-oriented moment, it carries traces of some of the secular and inclusive tropes of the former. As I have discussed elsewhere, the representation of the Mughal emperors in the ACK largely follows the post-Independence secular mode of history textbooks. The Mughal kings are not marked as invaders/outsiders even though they do not embody the nationalist manliness of ACK's iconic Hindu/Rajput heroes.[52]

Karline McLain's compares the final panels of *Shah Jahan* (1979) and *Shivaji* (1971): 'Shivaji is immortalized as the powerful warrior-king, seated gloriously on his golden throne before his bowing courtiers, while Shah Jahan is immortalized as a pathetic has-been, dreaming of the former days of glory as he lies dying.'[53]

I would argue that the ACK addresses not only the Hindu majoritarian constituency but also a more cosmopolitan, global sensibility that might identify with secularism and diversity (albeit divorced from thorny questions of caste and privilege). Even today, one finds a continuation of this tradition in the ACK venture—much after Pai. For instance, on 12 July 2023, the ACK website featured an article on the ghazal singers of India, including brief biographies of Mirza Ghalib, Dushyant Kumar, Sahir Ludhianvi, Nida Fazli and Javed Akhtar.[54] The ACK's distinctiveness lies in stitching together disparate sites and discourses—history and myth, secularism and Hindu nationalism, culture and modernity, and therein lies its appeal. It is important to look at the ACK not just as a cultural phenomenon from the past—as a nostalgia commodity—but to engage with its continuing influence on our hegemonic present.

Let me end with a brief reference to my more recent involvement with a project on stories that deal with marginalized childhoods, written by authors from marginalized groups. I am referring to my involvement in a project titled Different Tales: Stories from Marginal Cultures and Regional Languages, at the Anveshi Research Centre for Women's Studies, Hyderabad. The initiative entailed collecting children's stories from Dalit and other marginalized groups, outside the normative middle-class setting. The objective was to make visible stories that are rarely seen in print. Written in Telugu and Malayalam originally, these stories were translated into English and into both the regional languages. Different Tales resulted in a series of storybooks in 2008, mirroring the lives and aspirations of children from marginalized contexts in enabling and nurturing ways.

While collecting material and speaking to Dalit and Muslim writers from various regional contexts of Telangana and Kerala, we discovered that these stories often blurred the line between myth and history. However, unlike ACK, which was invested in an upper-caste, individualistic pedagogy, these aimed to create a sense of confidence and community in children from marginalized communities. For instance, noted Dalit feminist writer Gogu Shyamala rewrites the myth of the Tataki from Ramayana to allegorically portray the story of a little girl from the oppressed Madiga caste in Telangana, who dares to challenge the established land relations in her village.[55] Similarly, Shefali Jha's 'My Friend the Emperor' deals with how a Muslim child reconnects with the history of Babur, a figure that is routinely constructed as an 'invader' in mainstream (including secular) history.[56] The story draws on *Baburnama*, the memoirs of Zahir-ud-Din Muhammad Babur, to invoke the turmoils of his childhood after the loss of his father at the age of twelve and the subsequent family feuds over the throne of Ferghana.[57]

The pedagogic potential of history, as the Amar Chitra Katha has amply demonstrated, can be channelled to shape the politics of the present and the politics of the possible. But we need to explore how this potential may become part of our imagination of a more democratic and inclusive future—in the classroom, in children's literature and in our common sense.

NOTES

1 See Partha Chatterjee (ed.), *Wages of Freedom: Fifty Years of the Indian Nation-State* (New Delhi: Oxford University Press, 1998); Sumanta Banerjee, *In the Wake of Naxalbari: A History of the Naxalite Movement in India* (Kolkata: Subarnarekha, 1980).

2 It is interesting how Hindu-nationalist forces aligned with Jayaprakash Narayan's call for 'total revolution' in the 70s, seeking a 'complete reform of society inspired by Gandhi's ideals: the abolition of Untouchability and cast [*sic*] and, above all, an institutional transformation to make possible the primacy of society over the state, through the rehabilitation of politics at the local level' (Christophe Jaffrelot, *The*

Hindu Nationalist Movement and Indian Politics: 1925 to the 1990s [New Delhi: Penguin, 1996], p. 262). Editorials in the Hindu-nationalist press linked the idea with their own demand for spiritual revolution which posed as an alternative to the violent, Marxist-variety of revolution.

3   For an extensive analysis of this process, see Deepa Sreenivas, *Sculpting a Middle Class: History, Masculinity and the Amar Chitra Katha in India* (New Delhi: Routledge, 2010).

4   Gramsci describes three moments of political consciousness: (1) the primitive economic moment, when a group's own professional interests are expressed but it does not yet think of itself as a social class; (2) the political economic moment, when the consciousness of class interests surface but only at an economic level; and (3) the hegemonic moment, when the dominant

class realizes that their immediate interests need to be transcended to include the interests of subordinate groups. For Gramsci, this third moment is characterized by an ideological struggle which attempts to forge a unity between economic, political and intellectual objectives, when all struggle takes place around a 'universal', thus forging the hegemony of a fundamental group over several subordinate groups; see Chantal Mouffe, 'Hegemony and Ideology in Gramsci' in Chantal Mouffe (ed.), *Gramsci and Marxist Theory* (London: Routledge, 1979), pp. 168–204; here, p. 180. The concept of hegemony also involves intellectual and moral leadership, going beyond simple class alliance.

5   See Susie Tharu and Tejaswini Niranjana, 'Problems for a Contemporary Theory of Gender', *Social Scientist* 22(3–4) (March–April 1994): 93–117; here, pp. 95–96.

6   Tejaswini Niranjana, 'The Desire for
     Cultural Studies' in Meaghan Morris and
     Mette Hjort (eds), *Creativity and Academic
     Activism* (Durham, London: Duke
     University Press, 2012), pp. 25–40; here, pp.
     29.

7   Niranjana, 'The Desire for Cultural Studies',
     pp. 33.

8   Deepa Sreenivas, 'Transgressing
     "Innocence": Childhoods from the Margins'
     in Usha Raman and Sumana Kasturi (eds),
     *Childscape, Mediascape: Children and
     Media in India* (Hyderabad: Orient
     Blackswan, 2023), pp. 91–115.

9   Perry Nodelman, *The Hidden Adult:
     Defining Children's Literature* (Baltimore,
     MD: Johns Hopkins University Press, 2008).

10   From Rohith Vemula's suicide note, a
     searing indictment of the entrenched
     inequalities and casteism in academia and
     society.

11   Ajantha Subramanian, Introduction to *The Caste of Merit*: *Engineering Education in India* (Cambridge, MA: Harvard University Press, 2019).

12   Stuart Hall, *The Hard Road to Renewal*: *Thatcherism and the Crisis of the Left* (London: Verso Books, 1988).

13   Susie Tharu and Lalita K. (eds), *Women Writing in India*: *600 B.C. to the Present*, 2 VOLS (New Delhi: Oxford University Press, 1995), VOL. 2, pp. 108–9. Also see M. Madhava Prasad's discussion of the film *Mere Apne* (1971), where a widowed old woman brings together warring factions of disgruntled, unemployed youth, in *Ideology of the Hindi Film*: *A Historical Construction* (New Delhi: Oxford University Press, 1998).

14   The reference is to the famous motto of ACK, as coined by Pai: 'The route to our roots.'

15 Quoted in Jaffrelot, *Hindu Nationalist Movement*, p. 195.

16 It is important to view the ACK not as an isolated phenomenon but linked to and participating in the larger political/ideological battles to revision the past in order to build a *bharatiya* identity. Pai firmly believed that history was more than 'dates and facts', and that school history was ineffective precisely because it restricted itself to a dry, positivist idea of the subject. In a determined move away from this mode, he fashioned the ACK's history in the storytelling format, with illustrations becoming central to the project. Combining the Western comic style with pre-novelistic visual storytelling traditions of India—the chitra katha, scroll painting and fresco— ACK created figures that were simultaneously historical and contemporary, sacred and secular.

17 Anuradha Kapur, 'Deity to Crusader: The Changing Iconography of Ram' in Gyanendra Pandey (ed.), *Hindus and Others: The Question of Identity in India Today* (New Delhi: Viking, 1993), pp. 96–97.

18 Anant Pai, *The Role of Chitra Katha in School Education* (pamphlet) (Mumbai: India Book House, 1978).

19 For an extended discussion, see Deepa Sreenivas, 'Comics, Scrolls, Frescos and the "Chitra Katha" ' in *Sculpting a Middle Class*, pp. 43–81.

20 Yagya Sharma (script), Ram Waeerkar (illus.) and Anant Pai (ed.), *Padmini*, Amar Chitra Katha (Mumbai: India Book House, 1973).

21 Ramya Sreenivasan in her *The Many Lives of a Rajput Queen: Heroic Pasts in India, c. 1500–1900* (Seattle: University of Washington Press, 2007) writes about the

multiple narratives of the Padmini legend that have been in circulation since the sixteenth century. The earliest known version is Malik Muhammad Jayasi's *Padmavat* (1540) in Avadhi, a Sufi mystical adaptation of the heroic romances that were popular in the literary traditions in North India, portraying the dangerous quests undertaken by princes to court and marry women of legendary beauty.

22 Pai, *Role of Chitra Katha in School Education*.

23 Sudipta Kaviraj, *The Unhappy Consciousness: Bankimchandra Chattopadhyay and the Formation of Nationalist Discourse in India* (New Delhi: Oxford University Press, 1995), p. 111.

24 Yagya Sharma (script), Pratap Mulick (illus.) and Anant Pai (ed.), *Rana Pratap*, Amar Chitra Katha (Mumbai: India Book House, 1977).

25 As Ranajit Guha notes, '[T]he revolt of the
    1970s amounted to youth calling age to
    account' (in his introduction to *A Subaltern
    Studies Reader: 1986–1995* [New Delhi:
    Oxford University Press, 1997], p. *xii*).
    Alongside the nationwide questioning of the
    ruling party, the younger generation was
    eager to break away from a history it
    regarded as made up of utopian dreams and
    hollow promises.

26 Anant Pai, *How to Develop Self-confidence*
    (New Delhi: UBS, 1992), p. *viii*.

27 Partha, another name for Arjuna, indicates
    the way in which the child is addressed in
    this venture. Swami Chinmayananda's words
    in the introduction to *The Gita* are
    significant: 'Arjuna, a confused child of his
    age, is tenderly guided to rediscover in
    himself his own heroism. Lord Krishna
    expounds a healthy way of life which
    guarantees not only our worldly success in

life, but also ensures the ultimate unfoldment of man into the total perfection of Godhood.' Anant Pai (script and ed.) and Pratap Mulick (illus.), *The Gita*, Amar Chitra Katha (Mumbai: India Book House, 1977).

28 Anant Pai, *How to Achieve Success* (New Delhi: UBS, 1993), p. 11.

29 Pai, *Role of Chitra Katha in School Education*.

30 Partha Chatterjee, *Nationalist Thought and the Colonial World: A Derivative Discourse?* (New Delhi: Oxford University Press, 1986), p. 57.

31 P. Narasimhayya (script), Souren Roy (Illus.) and Anant Pai (ed.), *Adi Shankara*, Amar Chitra Katha (Mumbai: India Book House, 1974), p. 14.

32 Yagya Sharma (script), Ram Waeerker (illus.) and Anant Pai (ed.), *Chanakya*, Amar Chitra Katha (Mumbai: India Book House, 1971).

33 S. S. Rege (script), Dilip Kadam (illus.) and Anant Pai (ed.), *Babasaheb Ambedkar*, Amar Chitra Katha (Mumbai: India Book House, 1979).

34 Nandini Chandra, *The Classic Popular: Amar Chitra Katha 1967–2007* (New Delhi: Yoda Press, 2008), p. 218.

35 Suhas Palshikar, 'Toward Hegemony: The BJP Beyond Electoral Dominance' in Angana P. Chatterji, Thomas Blom Hansen and Christophe Jaffrelot (eds), *Majoritarian State: How Hindu Nationalism Is Changing India* (London: C. Hurst & Co, 2019), p. 107.

36 Aman Luthra, ' "Old Habits Die Hard": Discourses of Urban Filth in Swachh Bharat Mission and The Ugly Indian', *Journal of Multicultural Discourses* 13(2) (2018): 120–38; here, pp. 123, 126.

37 Success, consumption, social awareness/responsibility and middle-class

identity entwine in novel ways—not overtly deployed around an upper-caste identity. Manisha Anantharaman's 'Elite and Ethical: The Defensive Distinctions of Middle-Class Bicycling in Bangalore, India' (*Journal of Consumer Culture* 17 [2017]: 864–86) points out how, by adopting bicycling as a mode of travel, upwardly mobile, middle-class cyclists lay claims to being ethical actors and ecological citizens concerned about the environments. However, through the consumption of high-end bicycles and gear, their social identity remains exclusive despite adopting a mobility practice that is identified as lower class/caste and stigmatized in a social context where personal automobiles are emblems of respectability and property.

38 Srinidhi Murthy, '5 Women Environmentalists Of India', *Amar Chitra Katha*, 15 March 2021. Available online: http://rb.gy/teox1 (last accessed: 2 October 2023).

39 '5 Must-Reads For Eco-Warriors', *Amar Chitra Katha*, 15 December 2020. Available online: http://rb.gy/8ej4p (last accessed: 2 October 2023).

40 Uncle Anant, modelled after the founder of the series, educates children about the 'lost' history of waste disposal in India. He recalls how the 2,500-year-old Indus Valley Civilization led the world in 'sanitary engineering' and how the Vedas urged people to lead disciplined, hygienic lives. The narrative represents the Swachh Bharat mission as a 'new dawn' that awakens the 'old dream', after centuries of neglect towards sanitation. Reena I. Puri, et al. (eds), *Swachh Bharat: The Clean Revolution* (Mumbai: ACK Media, 2017).

41 Subramanian, Introduction to *The Caste of Merit*, p. 6.

42 Carol Upadhya, 'Software and the "New" Middle Class in the "New India" ' in Amita

Baviskar and Raka Ray (eds), *Elite and Everyman: The Cultural Politics of the Indian Middle Classes* (London: Routledge, 2011), pp. 167–92; here, pp. 175–79.

43 Darlington Jose Hector, 'Introduce an Amar Chitra Katha for Entrepreneurship and Wealth Creation at School Level: Hurun India Founder', *Moneycontrol* (18 October 2022). Available online: http://rb.gy/9u9f3 (last accessed: 2 October 2023).

44 T. V. Jayan, 'Amar Chitra Katha Opens New Page, on Corporates', *The Hindu BusinessLine*, 23 December 2019. Available online: http://rb.gy/zrn7q (last accessed: 2 October 2023).

45 *Atmanirbharta* is Hindi for 'self-reliance'. The phrase *Atmanirbhar Bharat* (Self-reliant India) has been popularized by the prime minister Narendra Modi, especially since the COVID-19 lockdowns.

46 MN4U Bureau, 'Godrej & Boyce
    Collaborates with Amar Chitra Katha to
    Launch a Book on the Life of Industrialist
    Naval Godrej', *MediaNews4U*, 26
    October 2022. Available online:
    http://rb.gy/sv35r (last accessed: 2 October
    2023).

47 Such a value system is marked off from the
    corruption of the earlier state-controlled
    economy, often referred to as 'license raj'.
    Further it is dissociated from the
    inheritance-based structure of an old
    business class.

48 Upadhya, 'Software and the "New"
    Middle Class in the "New India" ', p. 184.

49 Kajri Jain, 'Muscularity and Its
    Ramifications: Mimetic Male Bodies in
    Indian Mass Culture', *South Asia* 24,
    special issue (2001): 197–224; Kapur,
    'Deity to Crusader'.

50 Purnima Mankekar, 'Epic Contests: Television and Religious Identity in India' in Faye D. Ginsburg, Lila Abu-Lughod and Brian Larkin (eds), *Media Worlds: Anthropology on New Terrain* (Berkeley: University of California Press, 2002), pp. 134–51; here, p. 132.

51 Uma Chakravarti, 'Inventing Saffron History: A Celibate Hero Rescues an Emasculated Nation' in Mary E. John and Janaki Nair (eds), *A Question of Silence? The Sexual Economies of Modern India* (New Delhi: Kali for Women, 1998), p. 247.

52 See Deepa Sreenivas, 'The Muslim "Other": Figures of Evil and Charisma from Popular Visual Culture in India', *Tasveer Ghar* (available online: http://rb.gy/35v09; last accessed: 2 October 2023) for an extended discussion.

53 Karline McLain, *India's Immortal Comic Books*: *Gods, Kings, and Other Heroes* (Bloomington, IN: Indiana University Press, 2009), pp. 153–54.

54 Srinidhi Murthy, 'Ghazal Writers Of India', *Amar Chitra Katha*, 12 July 2023. Available online: http://rb.gy/31llv (last accessed: 2 October 2023).

55 Gogu Shyamala, *'Tataki Wins Again'* and *'Braveheart Badeyya'* (Puja Vaish and Rashmi Mala illus, A. Suneetha trans., Deepa Sreenivas ed.) (Kottayam: Mango Books, 2008).

56 Shefali Jha, Rekha Raj, *Spirits from History*: '*My Friend, the Emperor*' and '*Beloved Spirits*' (Deepa Sreenivas ed.) (Kottayam: Mango Books, 2019).

57 Notably, ACK's *Babur* (1977) too traces the Mughal emperor's childhood burdened with enormous odds (loss of parents,

invasion of his kingdom by deadly enemies, and so on) and his determined journey forward, to ultimately emerge as the 'Emperor of Hindustan'. However, a separate Muslim world order is signalled by the colour-scheme. For example, the elements in the panels—attires, plants, scenery, floors, walls—are suffused in shades of green.